Words for God's Daughters

By Reverend Sameerah L. Shareef

A 30-DAY DEVOTIONAL
FOR POWERFUL WOMEN ON THE MOVE!

©MAY 2020 SAMEERAH L. SHAREEF
ALL RIGHTS RESERVED

Chapbook Press

Schuler Books
2660 28th Street SE
Grand Rapids, MI 49512
(616) 942-7330
www.schulerbooks.com

Words for God's Daughters: A 30 Day Devotional for Powerful Women on the Move!

ISBN 13: 9781948237567

Library of Congress Control Number: 2020920014

Copyright © 2020, Sameerah Shareef

All rights reserved. No part of this book may be reproduced in any form except for the purpose of brief reviews, without written permission of the author.

Printed in the United States by Chapbook Press.

Dedication

Dedicated to all the QUEENS in my life, my daughter Queens, Ameenah and Nandi; my daughter in love, Tamorah; my best sister Queen friends, Landis and Pat, my "bio-sister Queens, Sylvia and Prosperity to my G-baby Queens and princesses, Crystal, Hanifa, Haniya,, Zion, Tahirah, Nasira and, A'laileana, Keh'lani, Z'havia all the other Sister Queens who continue to bless my life, you know who you are!

About the cover ...
The Iris flower symbolizes wisdom. It's what God gives freely if we simply ask!

A Devotional for God's Daughters! Introduction

There are three TRUTHS that are the foundations of this book.
1. All women are loved by God.
2. We are all God's Daughters.
3. We all can count on God to order our lives.

Our "DAUGHTER-HOOD" comes directly from our being of Divine Royal origins. We came from God, who is the Great Holy Royal One and since we are made in the image and likeness of God, "royal-ness" is part of our spiritual DNA! Scripture reminds us, *"But you are a chosen people, a royal priesthood, a holy nation, God's special possession, that you may declare the praises of God who called you out of darkness into Divine wonderful light."* 1 Peter 2:9 (NIV)

God claims us as Royal Daughters.

Being a Royal Daughter requires us to accept the responsibility, accountability, concerns and joys of living life as royalty. Living a royal life requires a lot! We all "daughter" in our lives whether we know it or not. Our "Daughter-hood" is simply how we handle our lives. How we live, how we act, or not, on the things that are a part of our lives. The ways that we respond/react to those life things that are within our area of reach and influence. It's about how we are experiencing our lives and how others experience us. No matter what, we are God's Daughters!

It's all about our effectiveness to handle our business, navigate the waters of our daily living and accomplishing what we were sent here to do by Royal Decree of our Royal creator. Being God's daughter is about impacting the world in positive ways. It does not mean dominating and wielding power over others. It does not mean living as a power hungry, power seeking tyrant. Get the fairy tales out of your head!

The truth is, Daughters, we can either "daughter-down" or "DAUGHTER-UP." It's entirely up to us. To "daughter down" is to live a life filled with negativity. To live below what we know we are capable of. To believe that God does not love us or desire us to be successful, happy fulfilled, enlightened, etc. To settle for the least in us and others when we know that God expects more and so should we! To "daughter-down" means living a life that creates and accepts chaos as normal.

To "DAUGHTER-UP" is to live in the most positive ways possible. It is to accept that God loves us completely and has the best plans and expectations for us and our lives. It means using our gifts for the good of ourselves and others. It means celebrating our accomplishments and those of others. It means living lives that influence others to live positive lives as well. We are powerful women and we impact the world.

How did I come to understand my royalty and how to "DAUGHTER-UP"? It was by desiring to know how to live in ways that were consistent with who I really am and why I am here. I would venture to say that the same is true for you!

I want to share a few of the things that did or did not work in my life. I would like to try and help more of us come into our "DAUGHTER-HOOD" sooner rather than later.

Let's make it simple. I will list a few of the things that work/worked or don't work/didn't work.

What works/worked for me:
- Knowing I am loved by God, ALWAYS, and standing complete in Christ
- Accepting responsibility for my life and how it is being lived
- Intact self-esteem
- Consistently caring for myself as I care for others
- Using my gifts
- Declaring boundaries
- Understanding my inherent WORTHINESS
- Shining (my own light) and Sharing it (supporting others light)
- Declaring LOVE as my default action and motivation

What did not/does not work for me:
- Forgetting/ignoring that I am loved by God and I am complete in Christ

- Not accepting responsibility for my life and how it is being lived
- Believing myself unworthy
- Low self-esteem
- Inconsistent or no self-care, especially as I care for others
- Not using my gifts
- Letting Stuff "slide"-Not declaring boundaries
- Snuffing my own light
- Throwing shade or water on others light
- Allowing hate to take root and rule my actions

DAUGHTER-HOOD requires a true love for God, self-discipline, and a desire to live an effective, fulfilling life! The best way to DAUGHTER-UP is to allow God to be the reason that you live. The best way to keep this state of being is to keep God first in your life. This devotional offers daily Scriptures, prayers and words of reflection for every Daughter everywhere! My prayer is that it will bless your life to DAUGHTER-UP as God intends!

BE BLESSED!
Rev. Sameerah L. Shareef, M.Div.

DAY 1

¹⁹ See, I am doing a new thing! Now it springs up; do you not perceive it? I am making a way in the wilderness and streams in the wasteland.
Isaiah 43:19 New International Version (NIV)

Devotion
Daughter, on this first day of a new month, be reminded that God gives us newness on a regular basis. We get a chance to start new. We get an opportunity to go forth in new ways. God gives us new ideas. God shows us a new road to travel and a new way to get to where we need to be. Sometimes it seems to appear out of nowhere. Isn't that what God promised? That it would spring up? Pray for the blessing of increased perception to see what God has for you. You are at the start of a new month. Depending on the calendar, there are 28-31 new days ahead of you. The blessing is that God has already gone ahead of you! In our Scripture today, God states that there is a way already being made in any wilderness you might encounter and that there will be water in any desert you might find yourself in this month. So, you have all that you need to move into this new measure of time, this new day and new month. You can move with confidence and with the assurance of Divine presence. Be determined to DAUGHTER-UP this month!

Prayer
"Lord, prepare your Daughter for this new time in her life. Give her perception to see the things you have for her life and the power to walk where you are leading! In Jesus' name, AMEN!"

Notes

DAY 2

¹¹ *For I know the plans I have for you," declares the LORD, "plans to pros- per you and not to harm you, plans to give you hope and a future.*
Jeremiah 29:11 New International Version (NIV)

Devotion
Daughter, it is important to make plans for your life. Yet there is the understanding that God has the best plan! Indeed, God has plans for your life and has declared that those plans are for you to have a life that is good and prosperous. When you are making plans for your life and figuring out how to REIGN, remember to seek God. Ask God what direction you should go in. Ask God to show you what steps to take. Ask God for power to do what needs to be done. Ask God about decisions that need to be made. Then, live in positive expectation of how your life will unfold. In each and every accomplishment, every obstacle that you overcome, every victory that you experience, every dark moment that you come through, remember that God always has plans for your good. Plans to increase your hope. Plans for your future where you will DAUGHTER-UP!

Prayer
"Lord, bless your Daughter with a heart filled with hope and faith that you always will provide and want the best for her life! Your plans for her are already in progress! In Jesus' name! AMEN!"

Notes

DAY 3

[13] For you created my inmost being; you knit me together in my mother's womb. [14] I praise you because I am fearfully and wonderfully made; your works are wonderful, I know that full well.
Psalm 139:13-14 New International Version (NIV)

Devotion
Daughter, there is power in realizing that you are KNOWN! Recognize that God knows you and knows you well! There is nothing about you that God doesn't know so you can rest with confidence in God's presence! Do you have someone in your life that knows you well? If you do, God knows you even better. If you think you don't, God knows you best of all! You can be 100% completely real and authentic with God. Being known in this way places you in a position to get exactly what you need for your life! As your creator, God knows where you need healing. God knows what your strengths are. God knows where you are most gifted. God know where, when and how to place new gifts in you! God knows how to grow you far beyond your beliefs about how much you think you can grow. You are a wondrous, unique creation of God. You have been that from your very beginnings! Be well aware of that, give God praise for it and DAUGHTER-UP!

Prayer
"Lord, remind your Daughter of how awesome she is and that you intentionally created her that way. She is known by you and that gives her meaning and power to live! In Jesus' name! AMEN!"

Notes

DAY 4

6-7 Don't fret or worry. Instead of worrying, pray. Let petitions and praises shape your worries into prayers, letting God know your concerns. Before you know it, a sense of God's wholeness, everything coming together for good, will come and settle you down. It's wonderful what happens when Christ displaces worry at the center of your life.
Philippians 4:6-7 The Message (MSG)

Devotion
Daughter, worrying and anxiety will steal the very life out of you! It will. It changes your whole body. It changes the way your body works on every level, physically, spiritually, emotionally, mentally. It will kill you! No one woman has enough "worry" inside her to cover all the things that could be worried about! So, in every situation and circumstance, you pray, give God praise and let God handle it. Keep moving as directed by God, through whatever it is, then turn your worry into prayer. Pray for guidance. Pray for enlightenment. Pray for relief of any pain you are having. Pray for whoever or whatever is stressing you out. Pray for release. Pray for resolution. Pray for peace. Pray for whatever it is that you need. Pray as you are moving through this day. Pray as you drive. Pray as you work. Pray at lunchtime. Pray when you get home. Go into God's presence wherever you are and pray. If needed, let your tears be your prayers. Send your moans up to God. Praying is one of the most powerful tools for a Daughter to use! Feel God's attention to your life and your situation. Know that God will move that worry from your center and you will continue to DAUGHTER-UP!

Prayer
"Lord, hold your Daughter close. Give your attention to her worries. Move them from the center of her being and place your peace there instead! Let her know that you have it all handled! In Jesus' name, AMEN!"

Notes

DAY 5

*⁵Trust in the LORD with all your heart
and lean not on your own understanding; 6 in all your ways submit to
the Lord, and the Lord will make your paths straight.*
Proverbs 3:5-6 New International Version (NIV)

Devotion
Daughter, you live a life filled with the need to trust and you do it every day in so many ways! You trust that your body will work, that your car will start, that the floor or pavement beneath you will hold you up as you walk. You trust that people are honest in their actions, interactions and transactions with you. You practice trusting every day. Sometimes, your trust is misplaced...it happens. The car doesn't start, you have pain in your body, there are cracks in the floor and potholes in the pavement...someone betrays you in some way. Scripture today reminds you to put the ultimate trust in God. Your understanding of any and all things is limited, no matter how brilliant you are...and you are brilliant! So, you are encouraged to put the greatest trust in the one that has all the answers. Whatever it is that you have to do. In all the things about you and your life, go to God for full understanding and directions. Your way will be made clear. You will know what to do and you will DAUGHTER-UP!

Prayer
"Lord, remind your Daughter that it is not required of her to know everything. That job is already handled by YOU! Let her know that you are the Creator of all that exists, and you DO know your way around this world. Show her the path you want her to take. Direct her in everything concerning her life. In Jesus' name! AMEN!"

Notes

DAY 6

²⁷ God created human beings; God created them godlike, Reflecting God's nature. God created them male and female.
Genesis 1:27-Message Translation (MSG)

Devotion
Daughter address any question in your mind right now about how God sees you in terms of your gender. You are not lesser to anyone, no matter what their gender might be! You were created in God's image, equal in the reflection of God you were given and entitled to all the rights and privileges of a child of God. The world in which you live may send you other messages. You might deal with all kinds of "isms" as you go along your journey. Sexism, Racism, Ageism, you name it, you might face it, but know your real "place" in all of it. God has made no distinctions in human creatures. You are equal to all! There are none that hold a higher place in God's heart. You are equally important, valuable, desirable, able, etc. as any other. Know that as a divine creature, you can walk confident in this truth. In the face of any that may try to tell you otherwise, stand your ground in this truth! Stand in your power! Stand in all your feminine power! Be royal in your femininity! Exude the aroma of womanly greatness that God has given you! Help to heal this world by being totally female, made in God's image, and DAUGHTER-UP!

Prayer
"Gracious God, by your wisdom, your daughter is female. Remind her that she is powerful in being all that you have made her to be, however she expresses her divine femininity. Remind her that you have placed equal value on all of your creation and that she can DAUGHTER-UP and do all that you have called her to do as your creation! In Jesus' name! AMEN"

Notes

DAY 7

⁴³ *But now, this is what the LORD says—God who created you, Jacob, God who formed you, Israel: "Do not fear, for I have redeemed you; I have summoned you by name; you are mine. 2 When you pass through the waters, I will be with you; and when you pass through the rivers, they will not sweep over you. When you walk through the fire, you will not be burned; the flames will not set you ablaze."*
Isaiah 43:1-2 New International Version (NIV)

Devotion
Daughter, how afraid are you right now? If you are doing ok, then how afraid have you been in the past? How much has fear ruled your life and made decisions for you? Fear is a part of the spectrum of human emotions. It is designed to get your attention, but it should not rule your life! There will be rivers, flood waters, turbulent waters, flames, fires and infernos but know that God is with you in it all. If you hold on to this promise, it will keep you steady when fear tries to rule. You must keep moving through all depths of the waters and all the varying degrees of heat that will show up in your life. As you go through the waters, remember that God has determined that fear in your life will not take you under. As you walk through the fire, remember that God has determined that you will not be consumed by your fear. GOD IS WITH YOU! By Divine grace, any fear can be dealt with. Some fears take a little longer to handle, but you have Divine power to do so! Feel the fear, Queen, then pray and keep moving forward! Fear cannot stand against you as you DAUGHTER-UP!

Prayer
"Gracious God, you know your Daughter's innermost fears. You know those things that keep her awake at night. You know those things that cause her to tremble uncontrollably. You know her deepest terrors. You know what brings the tears in her most desolate times. Touch her in her heart, ease her mind and calm her spirit. Remind her that she is in your Hands and she will come through! In Jesus' name! AMEN!"""

Notes

DAY 8

[29-31] *"What's the price of a pet canary? Some loose change, right? And God cares what happens to it even more than you do. God pays even greater attention to you, down to the last detail—even numbering the hairs on your head! So don't be intimidated by all this bully talk. You're worth more than a million canaries."*
Matthew 10:29-31 The Message (MSG)

Devotion
Daughter, you are precious in the sight of God. Great attention is paid to you, your well-being, your happiness, your deepest desires and the state of your soul. You are deeply cared for by your Creator! You are important to God and all things concerning you are God's concern as well. Your creation inside your mother's womb was done with great attention to detail. God wanted to make you unique...and you ARE! There is not another you, even if you have an identical twin. You bring to this world gifts, talents, abilities and a way of being that no one has ever brought before or will in the future. God cares about everything concerning you. God cares about the smallest thing that causes you concern and will give you all that you need to handle your life! Your contentment and satisfaction are on God's agenda. Your pain and anxiety are known as well and God can help you find relief. God has given each hair on your head a number. That level of care is what you need. So, don't be intimidated and made to think you don't matter and no one cares. Know that great care goes into who you are and who you will be. Your DAUGHTER-HOOD is surrounded by Divine care!

Prayer
"Gracious God, the best care of your Daughter has always been and will continue to be in your hands. Thank you for caring for her in ways that only you know how. Remind her how much you care for her! Remind her that the bullish ways of the world and the un- caring people she will meet should not dampen her spirit. You care for her and will continue to do so, always! In Jesus' name, AMEN!"

Notes

DAY 9

[20] *She opens her arms to the poor and extends her hands to the needy.*
21 When it snows, she has no fear for her household; for all of them are clothed in scarlet.
Proverbs 31:20-21 New International Version (NIV)

Devotion
Daughter, you are wearing so many hats! You play so many roles in your life and most of these roles involves caring for others. You do it so well. You are so good at it that people keep asking for more from you! You are gifted in so many ways. God has given you so much to share. Your light shines so bright that you have plenty of flame to light the lights of others. You attend to your home with care and in great detail. You meet the individual needs of your child(ren), knowing what they need in particular and how they need it. You budget and save so that your household is covered. Hard times may come but you are well prepared to weather the storm! You have a generous heart. You have a giving, nurturing nature. Your insight, intuition and "mother wit" make you a force to be reckoned with! You are willing to serve others and for this, God is grateful. You are a woman that lives with com- passion in the center of her heart. You hear the cries of those in need and you are ready to assist. Your caring creates groups, organizations, programs, and agencies that help meet the needs of our world. Your concern has built hospitals, homes, orphanages and other physical sites that heal and help millions around the world. A divine DAUGHTER lives best when everyone around her feels the warmth of her care.

Prayer
"Gracious God, you have given your Daughter a caring nature. Strengthen her as she cares for others. Remind her that as she cares for others, she is living out what you have called her to do. As she shares her gifts for the benefit of others, you are glorified, and you are pleased! What she does for the least of creation, she does for you! In Jesus' name, AMEN!"

Notes

DAY 10

[19] *"Do you not know that your bodies are temples of the Holy Spirit, who is in you, whom you have received from God? You are not your own; 20 you were bought at a price. Therefore, honor God with your bodies."*
1 Corinthians 6:19-20 New International Version (NIV)

Devotion
Daughte, your body is Holy. Your entire body...physical, mental, spiritual, emotional...in all the ways that you exist, it is Holy. The Holy Spirit, the Spirit of God resides in YOU! So, caring for your body, caring for yourself is important. It is honoring God when you take care of yourself. It is an act of worship! What? Yes, when you care for yourself, you are honoring God. It is not selfish or vain. You must take care of yourself. When you don't care for yourself, and you continue to care for others, you become depleted. Soon there is nothing left and you begin to do things that are unhealthy as a way to cope with the life you have built and allowed to be built around you. You become frazzled, stressed out, sick, irritable, angry, unhappy and can't figure out why. Honor God by caring for you. It must be intentional. It must be a part of what you do day to day, just like all the other important things you do day to day. It can be simple, and it should be enjoyable. Joyfully cleanse yourself daily with prayer, water, positive self-talk and loving caring interactions with others. Take a moment and remind yourself that God made you fabulous and taking care of that fabulous woman is important. How about looking in the mirror and saying, "Thank you, God, for creating wonderful me!" Healthy food, moving your body in ways that help it grow strong, getting sleep that restores you for the next day, words that encourage you and lift you up...all these things and other life affirming behaviors help to keep you in wonderful shape. When your total body is cared for, you DAUGHTER-UP in powerful ways!

Prayer
"Gracious God, thank you for the portion of the Holy Spirit that resides inside the body of your Daughter! Help her to care for and love her total self. Remind her how important she is to you and how important it is to care for the body/temple you have given her. Remind her to take time daily to do that and in so doing, she gives you glory! In Jesus' name, AMEN!"

Notes

DAY 11

² Be shepherds of God's flock that is under your care, watching over them — not because you must, but because you are willing, as God wants you to be; not pursuing dishonest gain, but eager to serve; 3 not lording it over those entrusted to you, but being examples to the flock.
1 Peter 5:2-3 New International Version (NIV)

Devotion
Daughter, you are a leader. Whether you acknowledge it or not, you lead! From your own household to the highest office known to human- kind. You were designed by God, to lead. As divinely feminine, the way you lead will not be like anyone else. Your life, your areas of influence require your leadership skills in the way that only you can provide. You are equipped to manage and move people forward whether it is yourself, your family, your community or all of these. You provide an example every day. People learn from watching you. What they learn from you is up to you! You were designed to be an example for those around you. The choice of what kind of example is up to you. God has placed inside you, the ability to care for others and to show them the way. You must seek God and listen for instruction as you lead. Be a willing leader. Accept the call that God has placed on your life. You are equipped. You have what it takes. You were placed in the world at this point in time to effect change in positive ways. Consider how you live in the presence of others. A good leader knows her strengths and areas that need improvement. A good leader acknowledges and seeks to improve any areas where growth is continuing. She is a work in progress. She grows and so will those around her. She pursues person- al excellence! Allow God to show you how to get the job done. When you lead, presenting before God and others your best, you DAUGHTER-UP!

Prayer
"Gracious God, you have created your Daughter to be a leader, whether it is her own family or a nation of millions. You have created her as a good shepherd able to care for a flock. You will lead her so that she can lead others. Give her courage to accept her leadership role and give her power to do so! In Jesus' name, AMEN!"

Notes

DAY 12

[14] "Because she[a] loves me," says the LORD, "I will rescue her; I will protect her, for she acknowledges my name. 15 She will call on me, and I will answer her; I will be with her in trouble, I will deliver her and honor her. [16] With long life I will satisfy her and show her my salvation."
Psalm 91:14-16 New International Version (NIV)

Devotion
Daughter, your protection is a Divine order decreed by God. There is protection to be found in the presence of God. Yes, you have probably experienced a time in your life where you felt far from protected! You may have experienced things that have harmed you. You may still be living in the aftermath of painful, awful things, yet you are a survivor. Where was the protection of God when you needed it? The clue is in the words, "I will be with her in trouble..." When you are going through it, God was and will be with you. You have the protection of God each and every moment of your life. It does not mean that trouble and pain will not come. It means that you have help and a way of coming through it all. You are God's Daughter. You have God's attention. Continue to love God and know that God intends to protect you. Pray and God will answer. Call on God and you will find a listening ear. Dare to pray for protection each day...protection for yourself, your family, your home, your community! Pray bold prayers for God to cover you in all areas of your life! Ask God for protection as you move through your life...every tri- al and every victory. Ask God to summon every resource available to come to your aid! As you, DAUGHTER-UP, God will be your protection!

Prayer
"Gracious God, you know all things concerning your Daughter and in that Divine knowledge, protect her in all her ways! Place a hedge of protection around her. Be her foundation. Have her back. Go before her and prepare her future. Be her covering each day. Let no hurt, harm or danger, seen and unseen overtake her! Grant her favor and ease in times of trouble and remind her of your presence with her even then. In Jesus' name, AMEN!"

Notes

DAY 13

⁶¹ Hear my cry, O God; attend unto my prayer. 2 From the end of the earth will I cry unto thee, when my heart is over- whelmed: lead me to the rock that is higher than I. 3 For thou hast been a shelter for me, and a strong tower from the enemy. 4 I will abide in thy tabernacle forever: I will trust in the covert of thy wings. Selah.
Psalm 61:1-3 King James Version (KJV)

Devotion
Daughter, in your time of distress, let a cry unto God be your first response! Let prayer be your first defense. Know that trying times will come. Know that the pains of life will visit you. Know also that you are God's Daughter and that you have a "rock" that extends far above what you are experiencing. There is no need to try and go through this time alone. God can be your shelter and your strength in all things. You may feel overwhelmed. It may seem impossible to handle. Others may tell you it's too late. You may be told no or no way. Overwhelming situations are God's special- ty! God is not overtaken by anything or anyone! God is a dwelling place that is safe and secure. God is able to sustain you! When you know where to turn in troubling times, your DAUGHTER-HOOD will be secure!

Prayer
"God, HELP! When your Daughter is going through distressing times, hear her cry and deliver her! Feel how overwhelmed she is and ease her pain. Lift her up and set her feet on sol- id ground. Help her to regain her balance and walk confidently through any and all situations! In Jesus' name, AMEN!"

Notes

DAY 14

^{1} The LORD is my shepherd, I lack nothing. ^{2}God makes me lie down in green pastures, God leads me beside quiet waters, ^{3}God refreshes my soul.
Psalm 23 New International Version (NIV)

Devotion
Daughter, all that you need, God can and will provide. God is a way maker. God wants you to have all that you need. God has created you to live and to have all that is needed in order to live. How many ways can it be said? God desires the very best for you and your life. Seek the source. For the smallest to the greatest need in your life, go to God! Perhaps you find yourself in need of the very essentials of life. Maybe you don't have all that you need. Maybe you don't see any way that you can get what you need. Remember nothing is too hard for God. Take a look around you. Take a look inside you. What has God given you that could be used to supply your needs? Maybe it's your gift of organization. Could you start a business organizing for other people? May- be it's your skill in the kitchen. Could you start a catering business? Maybe it's your people skills...you know how to talk to people, and they respond to you. Could you get some further training and work as a counselor? Maybe you have a natural ability to understand and use numbers and numerical formulas. Could you make your way into the world of engineering or accounting? God places in us the very means by which we can have what we need. Everyone has gifts, skills and abilities that can enhance their life. God gives us seeds to sow that will bear fruit! As you use those gifts, your DAUGHTER-HOOD will produce good fruit!

Prayer
"Gracious God, thank you for supplying all of your Daughter's needs. She has in her all that she needs. You are her source and you can make sure that she has whatever is required for her life. Remind her of the talents and abilities you have placed within her. Remind her that they are there for her to bear fruit that leads to a good life! You want that for her, and she can have it! In Jesus' name! AMEN!"

Notes

DAY 15

^{35} So do not throw away your confidence; it will be richly rewarded.
^{36} You need to persevere so that when you have done the will of God, you will receive what God has promised.
Hebrews 10:35-36 New International Version (NIV)

Devotion

Daughter, are you frustrated? No, really...are you frustrated? Have you been trying with all your might to get a particular thing done? Have you been working at this thing for what seems like forever and nothing is happening? Frustration is a part of every good thing that has ever been accomplished. What is this moment trying to tell you? Do you need to look at this thing in a different way? Perhaps you are trying to do this in your own strength and your strength alone. Ask God for more Divine strength to complete the work! Perhaps you should con- sider asking God if this is what you should be doing and if so, to show you who to reach out to for assistance. Your connection with other like-minded people is a great source of strength! Maybe you need to ask God for deeper insight into this thing...to show you another way of going at it. Maybe you should step back and find another way to view it. Frustration can be a test of your commitment. Don't lose your faith in the things God has called you to do! If you hang in there, the reward will be great! If you meet your frustrations with faith, you will DAUGHTER-UP successfully!

Prayer

"God, you see your Daughter. You see her facing yet another roadblock and she is ready to give up! Bless her with fresh insight into the situation. Help her to see another way to completing the task. Give her more strength for what needs to be done. Even show her a glimpse of what it will be like when the task is completed. She wants You to get the glory for a job well done! In Jesus' name, AMEN!"

Notes

DAY 16

18-20 After looking at the way things are on this earth, here's what I've decided is the best way to live: Take care of yourself, have a good time, and make the most of whatever job you have for as long as God gives you life. And that's about it. That's the human lot. Yes, we should make the most of what God gives, both the bounty and the capacity to enjoy it, accepting what's given and delighting in the work. It's God's gift!
God deals out joy in the present, the now.
It's useless to brood over how long we might live.
Ecclesiastes 5:19-20 The Message (MSG)

Devotion
Daughter you should be enjoying your life! God declared it! You are supposed to enjoy your life. You are to find all the joy possible in life. If you aren't enjoying your life, ask yourself why. Ask yourself what is keeping you from finding joy in your life. Ask yourself, "What am I waiting for?" The time to enjoy your life is NOW! If you are having trouble with this, try this strategy. Find one good thing every day and enjoy the goodness of that thing. It can be something as simple as the cool breeze on a very hot day. It can be the sound of birds singing their song in the morning. It can be the smile on the face of your loved one. Find it and enjoy it, then expand it to include another thing, then another and another until you find joy overflowing in your life! The ability to enjoy life is a gift from God that is given freely. Unwrap that gift in you and start using it! Enjoy the fruit of your labor. Enjoy the great results of your hard work. You deserve to enjoy life. God said so! As you rejoice and enjoy life, it adds sweetness to your DAUGHTER-HOOD!

Prayer
"God, your Daughter is working very hard. She is using the gift, talents and abilities you have given her, and she is bearing fruit! Help her to enjoy it. Help her to congratulate her-self and take delight in all that she is doing. Her life is her gift from You...she says THANK YOU! In Jesus' name! AMEN!"

Notes

DAY 17

¹³*"I can do all things through Christ who strengthens me."*
Philippians 4:13 New Revised Standard Version (NRSV)

Devotion
Daughter, have you ever been, or are you at, a point in life where you are questioning your abilities to do what you are doing? Or maybe, what you really want to be doing? Have you ever been told that you weren't "qualified" for a particular job or endeavor? Perhaps it left you questioning everything you thought about yourself and what you are supposed to do in life. You have been chosen for a particular assignment and only you can do it. Don't worry, you are more than qualified. You are more than equipped. You are the only one for the job. Many have tried to do this job, but it was intended only for you. You are to report for duty immediately! It is your life calling! God calls us first and then equips us. God has the ability to take us as raw materials and refine us to perfection for the task at hand! You are able to do all that your life is calling you to do. Not by your own power or strength but by the power of and standing in the strength of God! Whatever situation you are facing and whatever doubts are clouding your mind, be reminded that you can do those things that may seem impossible. God gives you the power to DAUGHTER-UP

Prayer
"Powerful God let your Daughter stand in your power for all those things in her life that seem impossible! Remind her of the victories already won and of her ability to win many more, through you. Remind her that you know her and will send her qualified for every task in her life. In Jesus' name, AMEN!"

Notes

DAY 18

²⁶ Blessed is she who comes in the name of the LORD.
From the house of the LORD we bless you.
Psalm 118:26 New International Version (NIV)

Devotion
Daughter, you are a blessed woman of God! You know that, right? You were blessed the day you were born! Blessed means you are sacred. You are connected to God. You are holy. You are set apart for divine purposes. Yes, you are blessed! Your life is blessed and everything that you set your heart, mind and hands to can be blessed. You must sim- ply claim your blessing by claiming the one who extends that blessing. God already speaks well of you. From the very heart of heaven, God speaks well of you (blesses) and declares you to be blessed and a blessing. Don't let the circumstances of your life determine how you view your life. You may have an abundance of material things but lack the spiritual insight to live in that blessing. You are rich but miserable. If so, ask God how to change your life. You may have little of what would be considered wealth but have the spiritual insight to know that is not where you are destined to remain. Come in the name of the Lord, meaning, live your life in the name of the Lord...in the ways of the Lord and the blessings will come! You are already blessed. You are blessed in every area of your life. You are so blessed that you are of benefit to others in your life. You are so blessed that your words heal souls. Your very presence shifts things and makes things better. You are so blessed that others look at you and wonder how to get where you are. Remember that blessings are not just material things. Blessed in your health, blessed with wonderful family and friends, blessed with joy and peace and an abundance of good situations in life. You are blessed! Look around as you DAUGHTER-UP and see how blessed you are!

Prayer
"Awesome God, your Daughter is so very blessed! Keep the blessings coming to her! Give her wisdom, insight and discernment to use those blessings to the good of herself and her world. Lord continue to speak well of her from heaven itself! In Jesus' name! AMEN!"

Notes

DAY 19

¹⁴The wise woman builds her house, but with her own hands the foolish one tears hers down.
Proverbs 14:1 New International Version (NIV)

Devotion
Daughter, your choice...be wise or foolish. You are a master builder. You have it in your spiritual DNA. God has equipped you with wisdom, knowledge, understanding, insight, discernment and ability to build the best house, the best life possible! You, you, YOU have what it takes to do what needs to be done! You can be wise enough; you ARE wise enough to make good choices. Handling your life, handling your business, being on your grind...whatever way you say it, is YOUR choice to make. Wise woman, each day you have a choice to do those things that build your house. Work smart, care for yourself, care for others, save and manage your finances, build a legacy for the future, give God glory by the way your house is built. Seek information and knowledge when you need it. If there is something you don't know, seek the answers. If something is out of order, ask for help in setting it right. Live in ways that build up your house. Don't let anyone or anything come in and destroy what God has blessed you to build. You could be your own worst enemy by living in ways that tear you down. You can align yourself with those who seek your destruction. You could fall into the trap of self-destruction. God is ready to assist you in construction of your home. God is already working on your behalf. Wise woman let your foundation be God and let your house be built as you DAUGHTER-UP!

Prayer
"Master Builder, your Daughter is ready to continue to build the awesome house you have equipped her to build! Be with her in the construction of every aspect of the building process. Let her house be a holy beacon, a safe peace filled place, a sacred space, a strong place in troubling times and most of all, let it be a testimony to your being in her life! In Jesus' name! AMEN!"

Notes

DAY 20

¹⁷ The LORD thy God in the midst of thee is mighty; God will save, God will rejoice over thee with joy; God will rest in his love, God will joy over thee with singing.
Zephaniah 3:17 King James Version (KJV)

Devotion
Daughter, God is so happy about being with you that Divine songs are created! Yes, God sings over you! You got your own tune that God has composed just for you! Yes, God is with you and Divine power comes along with that presence. God that is with you right now is powerful! It is in God's plan to keep your life in a good way. So, what is your response to this? Will you acknowledge God's presence in your life? Will you enjoy God's presence in your life? Will you be as happy to have God around as God is to have you around? You are a delight to God. You make God happy. That should make you smile today! You are never rejected by God. You can find forgiveness with God. You are totally accepted by God, even with your flaws, despite your mistakes, your decisions, your actions or failure to act. Don't let anyone convince you otherwise. God is with you, complete with your own theme song, as you DAUGHTER-UP!

Prayer
"God, keep the music playing in your Daughter's life! Let her hear the songs you sing over her. Let her feel the melodies from heaven that are sent daily to cheer her and lift her spirits. Remind her that you are happy to have her in your presence. In Jesus' name! AMEN!"

Notes

DAY 21

⁷ Be still before the LORD and wait patiently for God; do not fret when people succeed in their ways, when they carry out their wicked schemes.
⁸ Refrain from anger and turn from wrath;
do not fret—it leads only to evil.
Psalm 37:7-8 New International Version (NIV)

Devotion
Daughter you have carried it much too long. You have tried to handle it all on your own. You have studied it, cried over it, re-lived it, re- worked it...have you tried surrendering it? Have you considered giving it to the One who can handle anything? You can't stand another per- son getting ahead of you...getting the best of you...getting what you feel you should have. It seems that those against you are making progress in causing your downfall. You are sure that no one understands and certainly no one cares. Have you given it over to the One who has the blueprint for your life? How long will you go on allowing the burden(s) to weaken you? God is not unaware of what you are dealing with. God has not turned a blind eye or deaf ear to your situation(s). Try stillness...quiet time with God. Sit and cause your whole being to stop fighting with whatever it is.... sit and be patient before God. Resist the urge to allow the anger to consume you and provoke you to do something you will regret. Give it over to the One who knows your whole life story from beginning to the future. Your enemies will not overtake you. You will DAUGHTER-UP through this... God will make sure of it!

Prayer
"Sovereign God, you see your Daughter struggling. You know that she has tried to fight this battle on her own. Please remind her that you can handle it all, then lift this burden and give her peace of mind. Sure, she is strong, but you are stronger. She is a warrior, but you are the Victorious One! Fight this battle for her, in Jesus' Name, AMEN!"

Notes

DAY 22

⁸ But God's already made it plain how to live, what to do, what GOD is looking for in men and women. It's quite simple: Do what is fair and just to your neighbor, be compassionate and loyal in your love, And don't take yourself too seriously— take God seriously.
Micah 6:8 The Message (MSG)

Devotion
Daughter, some days it's all too much. Decision after decision. Every- thing seems so confusing. There seems to be no clear-cut answer to any question. It's seems unclear what the best course of action would be. How can anybody figure out what to do day to day? How do you live a good and Godly life? There seems to be so many rules and guidelines none of which make sense consistently. One day it's this thing that is morally correct. The next day it's changed to something different. At least it seems that way. Day to day living is challenging sometimes! God never intended for things to be this hard. The guide- lines have been consistent over time. Day to day living requires being fair and just to everyone... being compassionate as you live and love the people in your life and in this world...make love the consistent thing that fuels your life. It also requires a humble state of mind....one that puts God first. Your DAUGHTER-HOOD will be pleasing to God if you do so!

Prayer
"Loving God remind your Daughter of the "requirements" of being your child in this world. Give her continued integrity in her walk through this life. Give her clarity in the decisions she must make day to day. Help her to live up to Your expectations.
In Jesus' name, AMEN!"

Notes

DAY 23

[23] *The LORD makes firm the steps of the one who delights in the Lord;*
[24] *though she may stumble, she will not fall,*
for the LORD upholds her with a Divine hand.
Psalm 37:23-24 New International Version (NIV)

Devotion
Daughter, you have made, and you are going to make mistakes... or stumble. Living is like a dance that you are learning as you go. You know some steps very well because you have done that bit of choreography many times before. Then a new part of the dance comes along...your foot slips and you stumble. You make a mistake. Your steps are ordered by God who knows the whole dance. Who knows that you are more than capable of the dancing so God holds you firmly with a strong grip until you are back in step. Mistakes teach you the things that don't work. The movement that doesn't fit in the dance. Mistakes are not life sentences...they do not define who you are. The One who is directing the dance, directing your path through life is always ready to forgive and show you a better way. You are designed to acknowledge your errors, receive correction and keep moving. Your DAUGHTER-HOOD depends on it!

Prayer
"Merciful God, thank you for the forgiveness you extend to your Daughter! Thank you for new mercies every day for her. Thank you that you continue to guide her path after every stumble that may happen. Thank you for your strong hand that keeps her! In Jesus' Name! AMEN!"

Notes

DAY 24

⁴ Take delight in the LORD, and the Lord will give you the desires of your heart. ⁵ Commit your way to the LORD; trust in the Lord and the Lord will do this: ⁶ The Lord will make your righteous reward shine like the dawn, your vindication like the noonday sun.
Psalm 37:4-6 New International Version (NIV)

Devotion
Daughter, what is your hearts' desire? Maybe you have more than one. What are you still hoping for in your life? How do you get what you want? Beyond your day to day needs...the thing(s) that you deeply want? Think about God when you think about that thing or things. Think about the ways of God and the presence of God in your life. When you find yourself before God in prayer, it's ok to ask for your hearts' desire(s). God wants you to have joy in your life. God wants you to have those things you hold dear in your heart. God desires to bless you in that way. Oh yes, and in those ways that you have been wronged, God has a plan to show your innocence and righteousness to all that need to see it. Thought you should know that too! Remember that as you DAUGHTER-UP!

Prayer
"God, in your wisdom and according to your plan, give your Daughter the deepest desires of her heart! Help her rejoice in her place in your life. Help her to find joy in your presence. Remind her that her adversaries will not have the last word either! In Jesus' Name! AMEN!"

Notes

DAY 25

[7] "Now, get on your way quickly and tell his disciples, 'He is risen from the dead. He is going on ahead of you to Galilee. You will see him there.' That's the message." [8-10] The women, deep in wonder and full of joy, lost no time in leaving the tomb. They ran to tell the disciples. Then Jesus met them, stopping them in their tracks. "Good morning!" he said. They fell to their knees, embraced his feet, and worshiped him. Jesus said, "You're holding on to me for dear life! Don't be frightened like that. Go tell my brothers that they are to go to Galilee, and that I'll meet them there."
Matthew 28:7-10 The Message (MSG)

Devotion

Daughter, who is waiting on you to tell the message? Who is waiting to hear you say that God will meet them? Didn't you know that you had the responsibility to minister to others? You have a ministry! God wants to accomplish something wonderful through you. Something life giving...something exceptional and excellent. Please don't limit your thinking to the ministry done from pulpits all over the world. For most women, their primary ministry is their family. The people that you impact day to day. (Of course, it is not limited to that. Perhaps God is calling you into a larger territory.) You have much good to accomplish. That is what ministry is. It is about increasing the good in the world and reminding everyone of God's love for them and the Divine presence in their lives. You have done and will continue to do good work. God has a ministry that is designed just for you. As you DAUGHTER-UP, the results of your ministry will bear witness to God!

Prayer

"Dear God, you have placed your Daughter in this world to accomplish what you want. You have made her with a particular ministry in mind. Show her clearly how to move in that calling so that those who need to come to know you, will do so through her! In Jesus' Name! AMEN"

Notes

DAY 26

⁸Let the morning bring me word of your unfailing love, for I have put my trust in you. Show me the way I should go, for to you I entrust my life.
Psalm 143:8 New International Version (NIV)

Devotion
Daughter, there is a Divine direction for your life. If you feel that you are off course, ask for further instructions! God does not want you to think you are lost. (After all, God always knows where you are.) Yet, you are very much human, and the world has a way of providing distractions and interruptions that throw you off track. Each new day brings the reassurance of God's love for you. Place your trust in God...all of it! Believe that God will provide the right directions. Much like the GPS that you may have come to rely on, God can provide clear instructions on how to get where you need to go. (Actually, God is much better than GPS. When you have created the universe, there are no "dead zones" where the satellite won't work!) Yes, it can be very scary to turn over your entire life to God. You have worked hard to handle the things concerning you. Yet, remember that God has planned for you to be here from the very beginning. Your presence is not an accident and your destiny is not a mystery to God! In order to DAUGHTER-UP you must have a leader that knows the way!

Prayer
"Loving God, thank you for establishing the path of your Daughter! You provide direction and insight through every curve, hill, valley, dry place or rough waters. You know where the pleasant resting places are and where the fullness of her life resides. Continue to lead her to the place called her destiny! In Jesus Name! AMEN!"

Notes

DAY 27

⁹ There remains, then, a Sabbath-rest for the people of God;
¹⁰ for anyone who enters God's rest also rests from their works,
just as God did from Gods'.
Hebrews 4:9-10

Devotion
Daughter, you may rest. If you need permission, know that God says it's ok to do so! You need to rest. With all the great work you are doing, your human body needs time to regroup. You need a Sabbath that does not mean stopping some of the work you are doing and putting that time and energy into another area of work. It means a rest that is a temporary halt to all work. You need time and space to allow all of you to be at ease. When was the last time you did this? Really, really rested, from everything? A "Godly rest" if you will. Not going on vacation where everyone rests but you because you are caring for them the whole time. Not a time away where you pull out your laptop/tablet/electronic workstation to catch up on a few things. No, a real rest where nothing is required beyond the basics of feeding and cleaning yourself. (You can hang out in a jogging suit or yoga pants and a T-shirt) A rest where your mind can tune in to God's frequency and get connected again. A rest where you can enjoy your own company as well as God's. A rest where you can appreciate the wonders of nature. Rest is important to keep you whole, healthy and centered. Your DAUGHTER-HOOD depends on a well-rested you!

Prayer
"God of the Sabbath, clear space and time in the life of your Daughter so that she may rest! Show her the value of really resting and allowing you to refresh her. Remind her that she needs uninterrupted time with you...to enjoy you and your creation. She deserves it! In Jesus Name! AMEN!"

Notes

DAY 28

[11] *I have told you this so that my joy may be in you and that your joy may be complete.* [12] *My command is this: Love each other as I have loved you.*
John 15:11-12 New International Version (NIV)

Devotion
Daughter, JOY is yours! You have it because God said so! You have complete joy...nothing lacking, nothing missing and nothing/no one that can take it away. That inner peace that resides no matter what your circumstances. It's yours for the asking. It is dependent on two things; loving God and loving others (including yourself) as God loves you! Joy, that unshakeable kind. The kind that exists even in the middle of chaos and confusion. Why would Jesus give that kind of Joy? Jesus knew what you would be facing as you live your life. Jesus knew that only real joy would sustain you. You need joy for the hard times and also for the good times. It is joy that will help you enjoy all the good that your life has to offer. Joy makes your heart continue to love even when it has been broken. Joy is what encourages you to extend your table when God blesses you with a huge harvest. It's the incredible feeling that despite all that is challenging in the world, you still have a desire to DAUGHTER-UP for God's glory!

Prayer
"Oh God, full of Joy, continue to pour out your joy on your Daughter. Let her experience an ever-flowing river of Joy in her life. Keep the Joy coming and help her let it overflow into the lives of others! In Jesus' Name! AMEN!"

Notes

DAY 29

[33] *"I have told you these things, so that in me you may have peace. In this world you will have trouble. But take heart! I have overcome the world."*
John 16:33 New International Version (NIV)

Devotion
Daughter, where do you find your peace? Is it in the quiet hours before you go to sleep? Is it in soft music playing? Is it soaking in a nice tub? These are all good things. Yet, real lasting peace can only be found in God. Troubles come in all forms and from all different directions. Disagreements, upheaval, struggles, fights, pain, loss... it all comes your way at some point in time. Relief from the troubles of the world comes through this Divine peace! Jesus said that He has overcome the world. He knows all about it and has figured out how to conquer it. As a Daughter of the Divine One, you get to have this peace whenever you need it! God will give you the courage you need to face and conquer the world and the peace that you need to do it. Peace is a characteristic of one who will DAUGHTER-UP well! Seek God's peace!

Prayer
"Peace giving God, may your Daughter know that your peace is part of her Divine inheritance! Bring peace to her spirit right now! Settle any places of upheaval in her life. Fill her heart with peace. Give her unshakeable peace as she goes forth to overcome in her world. In Jesus Name, AMEN!"

Notes

DAY 30

[10] For we are God's handiwork, created in Christ Jesus to do good works, which God prepared in advance for us to do.
Ephesians 2:10 New International Version (NIV)

Devotion
Daughter, you are at the end of the month! You have made it through and with the help of God you have done good works! Look back on the month and see all the things you have accomplished. Look at the Holy work you have completed. You were created by God with the ability to get things done. Celebrate each accomplishment, big or small! Celebrate each victory and every difficult situation you have come through. Take notice of what worked well. Also, take note of what did not, so that the next time around you can get the victory sooner! God has equipped you to do good works. Notice that the word is "works... plural... more than one! :-) God created you to be successful. It is in you to complete good works on a regular basis! Don't be surprised at the favor you will find as you do the works that God prepared for you. As you stay in step with God your DAUGHTER-HOOD will be filled with success!

Prayer
"Creator God, thank you for providing your Daughter with all that she needs to do the work you have called her to do! She is such a beautiful creation! Thank you for blessing the world with her presence. You know those things that she is capable of, now bless her with continued success! In Jesus' Name, AMEN!"

Notes

POSTSCRIPT

The most important relationship any woman can have is her relationship with God! No other relationship yields more positive benefits for her! God wants all women to understand how important, valuable, necessary, and vital they are to the world.

This book is a reminder to all women that God is interested in your life and wants you to have an abundant one! Read the words and be reminded of God's love for you. Read them every month, and it will be a source of inspiration to you!